Near and Far at the Beach

Learning Spatial Awareness Concepts

Amanda Boyd

I0809656

Math for the REAL World™

Rosen Classroom™

New York

This boat is near.

This boat is far away.

This boy is near.

This girl is far away.

This bird is near.

This bird is far away.

Words to Know

bird

boat

boy

girl